Pressed Flowers

Ashley Lazarz

For Tita

Introduction

A journey through life unfolding over and over again.

When I was asked as a child, "What do you want to be when you grow up?" my answer was simple: "Happy." Over time, I've come to realize that to know true happiness, one must also know sorrow, gloom, and darkness. Without sadness, there is no laughter. The complexity of this mutual dependence is something I have come to appreciate. As the months go by, and sadness creeps in, I know it is not permanent. The pain will not linger forever. Bliss and happiness will return. And once they do, the appreciation for belly laughs becomes unlike any other.

Vulnerability. I first trusted my pen and paper. Then, people came after. For so long, I felt alone in this world. I kept giving myself to others, hoping something or someone would stick. In the process, I completely lost myself. I lost those I loved deeply and effortlessly. My passions faded. I forgot what it meant to even identify them. Joy became an unfamiliar feeling. The world got smaller and lonelier.

Change had to happen, or my life would have no meaning. It would feel bleak.

December marks the hope for that change. Over the following months, I experienced connection, falling in love, dreaming, heartbreak, depression, self-love, and finding my true identity. Today, there are more genuine smiles and laughs than ever before. I believe everything will always work out the way it's supposed to. Today, I know I'm not alone and have found peace among the trees. I have finally thrown away the mask I kept in my back pocket for years. I am simply able to be me.

My hope is for you to find the hope within these words. To feel and relate to the deep emotions transcribed. To remember: it will be okay. My hope is that you allow yourself to smile as you read, and cry as you flip the pages. My hope is that you, too, are able to be a little more you.

Contents

I. December, hope   1

II. January, rebirth   18

III. February, lust   35

IV. March, body   54

V. April, connection   66

VI. May, dreams   78

VII. June, falling in love   93

VIII. July, depression   115

IX. August, heartbreak   133

X. September, self   150

XI. October, nature   169

XII. November, identity   185

December

December 28

Embracing my own company
I don't need you to dance with me

An abundance of flowers
As my depression begins to cower

When black has a new meaning
It's the story of healing

Bubbles

42 degrees
Eleven fifty three
I stare at you
You stare at me
How pretty you can be
Laying there so comfortably
Knitting my cherry blossom tree

Teaspoon

I never understood what happiness felt like until now
So stuck in a predetermined program I was forced into

It's like I finally
Stepped out of the line filled
With all of these complex robotic beings
Seeing oh so clearly,
This was not for me

It's not about how much money I make,
How many friends I have

It's about the little things
The music
When the butterfly sings

Our existence is unmeasurable;
But for what I can measure,
I want to make it worthwhile

I Promise You

Oh darling, I know
There are better days ahead
Just keep your chin up

Gift

The sun from above is on my skin
Defrosting the sadness from within
The permanent frown no longer here
Gifts arriving softly with the wind

With joy there is sorrow
Understanding one and the other
Appreciating both colliding worlds
Time and time again borrowed

They say to live in the present
Create your own colorful heaven
There is an abundance of beauty
Look around, take a deep breath in

Forage for an everlasting growth
Life wrapped and tied in this meaningful bow
The gift of delight and sadness
That is just the way life goes

Hope

In this confusing thing we call life
I try to fertilize the flowers and be polite
A little goes a long way
Why don't you give it a try?

I hope one day you begin to realize
It doesn't cost anything to be nice
This world could be a magical place
You may even be surprised

December 30

Will you come to my picnic
When the delicate snow has lifted
Tea and honey
It's almost like things have shifted

The earth has been singing
For oh so long I've been dreaming
Opening my eyes
What a beautiful feeling

A new perspective on love
Intangible wonders from above
Thank you for showing me
I have a purpose because of

Sit down under the sun
Picnic basket full with room for everyone
Possibilities
Our lives have just begun

Pacific

We don't have to know
Where we are destined to go
Step by step
Things will begin to show

Tornado of emotions
Just going through the motions
Please stop for a second
And listen to the ocean

I Wonder

Hello
I'm looking from afar
A field of wonders
Inside of your mind,

I wonder
If I'll ever feel a love
Greater than yours

I wonder
If you love me the way I do
A rooftop
A lovely creature approaching

I wonder
If I'll ever be able to explain
This
This
Or This

Questions

Sitting quietly in contemplation
Arriving just on time to the red station
Newspaper resting under my arm
Where is my new location?

Time traveling on this fast train
A train of the most insane
I saved you a seat
None of us are tamed

The world keeps flying by
Wanting to hold on tight
But I must let it all go
Leaving the grasp behind

An open fist
Why do we exist?
Contemplation hour
Hidden in the fine print

If only
Curated by madman
It is
We must live

Loafer/Heavy

Upon the gravel it lays
Trust in the soles of the universe
Basking in the summer rays
This is where we become two lovers

Fred once told me
It's time to be brave
No longer feeling so heavy
Utilizing lavender as my aid

Prescription

She used to be scared of change
Began to realize there is so much to gain
She wasn't ever truly happy
In her lingerie snorting cocaine

Hair tangled in spider webs
Guilt baked deep in the bread
She ate every crumb
And lit her third cigarette

Nothing but a skeleton
Thinking she was in her element
Life had to be more
She longed for a different type of medicine

Tomorrow

I made you this bouquet
To make sure that you are okay
The world must appear so gray
I promise tomorrow is a new day

December 31

This is it
The moment when I put me first
The moment when my body thanks me
The moment when my mind settles
The moment when the outside world is quiet
The moment when laughs become genuine
The moment when crying heals
The moment when creativity takes flight
The moment when love arrives without expectation
The moment when the wind moves through my skin
The moment when plants grow as I do
The moment when I start to feel fulfilled
The moment when opinions doesn't deter my growth
The moment when music soothes my soul
The moment when I feel sublime
This is it

But you can do it
Just because you haven't
Doesn't mean you can't

January

Memoir

Writing a story
A tale to entertain
In all of my glory
And a little pinch of fame

Creating this picture
Cutting and editing
Keeping the wild adventures
And all of the shedding

A story of hope
Love and adore
I hope you like the show
Go grab your popcorn

Innocence

My first breath
A little spec
Beautiful
Pure
More than enough

Swaddled from danger
Everyone is a stranger
A little baby
Not suited
For this is a corrupted life

Disco

Tricked out pants
A brick wall
She is already jumping over
Navigating a journey to crawl

Fifteen feet
Required ladder of peace
Outward gave grains
While she danced to the beat

Fourth Course

Coastline of the earth
Dainty electrons rebirth
Absorption into stars
All and everything you are worth

Freedom lingers for eternity
Peace is the new commodity
Finally arriving home
Pain sitting in her poverty

Magic beyond research
Gravity no longer returned
Floating into serenity
Tasting Heaven for dessert

January 11

Undertone of calm
Lizards waving in my palm
A body of zen
My safe haven I clearly saw

Movement so pure
A warrior in the mirror
This journey I embarked
It never felt more dearer

Beginning at one
Passion that can't be undone
So come with me
To a nirvana under the sun

White

A spirit of awe
Belief in something great
Greater than myself

Maker

I spend time with you
Alone with my thoughts in my room
Letting you speak through me
Asking for any type of clue

I usually don't know where to go
Or if on Sunday it will snow
I simply must trust
That guidance is what you will bestow

Simple Pleasures

Just to escape
Of all this and that
I get my acrylic paint
And draw circles over black

Gardening on Monday
Repotting for new experience
Whatever they may be
Eyes open and curious

Poem after poem
Mind therapy in the soul
Higher and lower
Journey only I know

Simple things that bring me joy
To form and reshape
Hibiscus La Croix
Just to escape

rebirth

Life is a rollercoaster

      And you just have to throw your hands up

Rebirth

It all once was lost
Sketched only because
Completing could be caught
What remained empty thoughts

Somewhere near
Or somewhere far
She held out her arm
In case it all began to fall

Grabbing it in the dark
A blind winter mark
Left on her cold shoulder
Umbrella under renaissance

January 19

A frolicking being
In a forest of feelings
She didn't quite know
Where the path was leading

Skip after skip
Branches opened into this
A mystical world
She jumped and took a dip

These enchanted waters
Indigo and lilac flowers
There she was greeted
By the most highest power

She took his hand
Serenity only she could understand
Peaceful they walked
Into the most promised land

Unit B

This is my chosen home
The front door is unlocked
Oh how I have grown
From such a dark spot

I couldn't have done it without you
Thank you deeply Elija
But I must go soon
So this is goodbye for now

Reincarnation

My body is beautiful
It carries my soul
Walking along this planet
Giving up all control

There is a deeper meaning
The meaning of life
To another dimension
Please pass me the knife

Cutting through the layers
We all seem to show
Who even am I
And where did she go?

Castles

If somebody told you I'd be here, now
I'd laugh and think you were joking somehow

Wild adventures has led to this
This single moment sweet as a kiss

I feel like I'm five again swinging in the air
So carefree, genuine, no longer thinking life isn't fair

I'm happy the old days didn't work out as planned
Like that one time I got lost sitting in the sand

I realize now it's all meant for a reason
It's all up from here, let's remain in this season

rebirth

Freedom

Breaking away now
Chain link falling from my wrists
I am free at last

Poetic resurgence

February

Skin

Lingering love
I feel his goosebumps
Touch mine

Glance and smile
Can you stay a while?

Tornado Dreams

I shouldn't be dreaming of you
You sweeping me away like the tornado wind
But there was no tornado
Just me and you making out in the bathroom

I didn't want to wake up from this dream
Because you made me feel so good
You grabbing my hair and biting my neck
It's like we knew this wasn't allowed
But we did it anyways

Now when I see you
I think of that dream
And I sometimes wonder
If someday it won't just be a dream

Pressed Flowers

Free will didn't make her free
Patiently waiting for the sea
Dissolving the crave
Of their history

She pressed the flowers
Valentines
Opening her white journal
It wasn't time

Illusions of feathers
Crunched between their cheeks
The feathers swallowed
Nonexistent for weeks

Gallon

This taste lingers
The taste of your fingers
Lemonade saliva
Let our bodies commingle

Vulnerable

Underneath this white woven blanket, I invite
you to meet all of me. Letting the infamous
guard of mine down is not a light occurrence.
I believe with my pounding heart that you
trust that I trust, I trust that you trust.
Take me, but leave a little for the bees.

Watercolor

Your voice thick with love
You are the best piece of art
No wonder they stare

Saturday Steve

I adore this city
A persuading mystery

You let me take over the aux
A DJ of your enormous heart

Symphonies and static
Replaced by plugged in magic

Driving barefoot under the moon
Engulfed in smells of sex and perfume

Treasure

The candles are melting
While our bodies burn together
Fire, lips are swelling
Show me all of your treasures

Hands

Your fingers dance on mine
Holding them very close this time
I never want to let you go
Picking the thorns off the vine

An electricity so evident
Admiration I have only dreamt
Keep holding on
You, I could never forget

75 mph

On this typewriter
Word after paragraph after chapter
I will write my thoughts
So we can make love after

Zealous passion unlocked
In the backseat of your black truck
Drive a little faster
Your love has gotten me drunk

Lust

Our blood begins mixing as one
An amalgamation of desires and the sun

Vampire teeth digging deep my neck
While everything starts falling off the desk

Hand grasped wrapped around my throat
Passion and gentle pain invoked

Bondage of intense infatuation
A beautiful lust intoxication

Satin

Over and over
You slip off my dress
Kissing my shoulder
Our bodies pressed

Your tender touch
Caressing my neck
I can't get enough
Our love so complex

Craving your energy
Your passionate being
I'll hold on to this memory
This fiery feeling

Dessert

Let me be your carnivore
Consuming your entire being
Constantly craving more
I kind of like it better when we're sloppy

Messy is our magic
Ending up on the floor among our clothes
Not locking the door is like a habit
Let's face it, we put on a pretty good show

The excitement of you naked
My body pressing on yours
I'm getting exhilarated
Can we go for round four?

lust

You smeared my red lipstick
And I was so okay with it

Jazz

We hit every red light on the way to our destination
Is the world trying to tell us to slow down?
Or is it giving us time to make out over and over again?

February 22

The world is quiet
All I hear is rain outside
I can't deny it
Trust me, I've tried

An irresistible love
For you and your body
Your pants become undone
Deep breaths are starting

My body melts on your skin
Sweat bleeding from our pores
Harps and violins
In this intense romantic orb

Sincerely

As you turn to me
Your hair gracefully kissing your cheek
Feeling your eyes pierce my soul
Inching closer as the bed squeaks

You put our favorite album on
The vinyl that you took from your mom
Intimate strings dance around us
My heart is racing while I am calm

Wearing the shirt I got you for your birthday
And the shorts with that small rip and fray
A quiet color story on your body
About to be loud as you make me your prey

Saving the leather for later
A delicate moment we cherish together
Making love under your dark blue sheets
Something of a love letter

Can you do that again?

March

Useless bones

10¢

I didn't let you in
Couldn't allow my vulnerability to win
Kept the knots tight
In my braid of leftover fringe

Found scraps all over the ground
While I tried to find sanity among this sound
Where do I even start?
When my keys aren't anywhere to be found

Could you drive this time?
I don't want to be left behind
I'll pitch in some gas money
But all I can find is this dime

Dysmorphia

I can't keep looking this way
Reflection of sick
You can't make me eat today
Body gaining too quick

I hide from the distorted mirrors
Run away from my jeans
Simply seeing horror
Since I was only fourteen

A comparing game
To the girls beside me
Never fitting the frame
Drinking starvation tea

Hoping and wishing
Maybe one day I'll see
That nothing is missing
And love me for me

Mask

Suffocated in cloth
Large black drapery
The style of a goth
Consuming sad royalty

A hard exterior
Plastered on this thin shell
Always felt inferior
I mean, can't you tell?

body

I wish I looked like that

Deserving

I know this world is messed up
Mistreated and corrupt
I never understood how
I ever deserved your love

Falsities

An orchestra of thoughts
Tainted teardrops
Following in the footsteps
Of a monster paradox

How could he love me
In this broken unwoven body
I never showed him
I remained a mystery

Noise

There is music in the background
Music in my head
I can never really tell which sound
Is trying to get fed

Cubed

You said I was pretty
I never believed it
The need to be skinny
Always hungry and disgusted

When you stopped looking
I consumed more ice
Invisible seasoning
Put it on twice

The formula of weight
The scale never lied
More and more hate
Coming from deep inside

Low

I hate this feeling
Of hating myself
This tornado of a being
Never asking for help

Comfortable in chaos
Wrapped in a dark cold blanket
I could write a whole essay on
The many ways I fake it

If I showed you how I felt
Then I would have to see me
Being honest with myself
That could never be

Change the way you see things

And things will begin to change

April

Spark

A mirrored distant reflection
Eyes locking in trajectory
Immediate luring connection
Feelings of innate ecstasy

Our initial hello
Coffee sips and late night drives
Turned to us on your pillow
Instantaneously mine

Jackie

Us and the green Jeep
Living wild and carefree
Borrowing your black dress
That night I turned eighteen

I'm happy these memories I have
Remind me friends help navigate the path
I'll listen to our song
And smile when I think back

Love, Kitty

Graffiti park
Just a little bit
Two twins from Mars
With an unstoppable fit

The planet couldn't take us
A force so strong
A bond beyond matter
Even while you've been gone

You & me against the world
Reuniting again
Nectar from the heavens
Dancing to Sebastian

So many memories
Years we can't undo
I'd do anything to go back
To a moment with you

I miss my best friend
Hot chili pepper
I know I'm not alone
Forever together

Nail Polish

You invited me over
To your comfy little space
Our bond getting closer
I brought coffee just in case

It's chilly outside
Jazz playing in the background
Vulnerable cries
Is there a tissue around?

Just two cool chicks
I feel like I've known you for years
Blossoming friendship
Holding it very near and dear

Right Here, Right Now

Human connection
Nurturing the imperfections
I want to lift you up
Feel this moment begin

Smell the beauty of the trees
Feel our voices become free
Take my hand
You are where you're supposed to be

I know you are scared of change
The mystery behind the flame
Let your courage shine through
You don't have to be afraid

We are all rooting for you
You'll be surprised what you can do
This is your time
Here is your breakthrough

Yellow

Yellow is the color of connection.
Bright, simple, energizing.
Like the warm sun hugging my skin.
The strangers that pass by.
I think of them wondering if they feel the same
energy as I.
A pulling energy encouraging one to smile.
Kindness is connection.

Annabel

Do you remember when I ran out of gas in an
unsafe place and you said, "Ashley, I'm here.
It'll be okay."

Connected

Everything is standing still
Like the calm lake waters upon the hill
Contentment felt
Between the blocks I have built

Beauty surrounding
Friendships climbing
I have found my people
Love unbinding

The hippies and the babes
These wild free humans
We're all here to create
Absolving the solution

Energy

The music is over
The lights are on
The glitter has fallen
But we're still dancing

A Forever Friend

I hold our friendship close
Like a flower standing against the wind
A little butter on the toast
Grateful I can call you a friend

It isn't easy for me to be open
To share thoughts and deep secrets
But you helped me become unbroken
And step into my uniqueness

Thank you for letting me grow
Letting me cry on the phone at night
For making late night cookie dough
And being a friend I don't have to rewrite

connection

They say, "friends come and go"
But why have you stayed?

May

Quill

There are many dreams locked away
Goals I want to achieve some day

Little baby steps I begin to take
Like holding my daddy's hand at eight

Hoping and wishing will only get me so far
I must pick up the feather and dip it in the jar

Moth

In this land of make believe
I wonder why the sky is green

Petals made of hands
Grasping for their romance

The ocean filled with crystals
Upon the queen they call

Show them your madness
Give them sweet violence

For it is us who slay
The monsters who betrayed

After it's all over
And the wind moves a little slower

The queen sits and drinks her tea
Among the moths, her beautiful company

dreams

Leave your soul in your backpack

Freddo

Drummer in the streets
Unconsciously speaks
A magnitude of inspiration
I so desperately need

In a trance of stirs
Flutists in the back heard
Asked to bring a melody
While the man speaks his word

Purple light correction
Peripheral interception
A cluster of creatives
Drowning in reflection

One day I'll be brave
To go up on that stage
For just right now
I'll gladly be entertained

Forest

Werewolves surround in the blind howls
Ubiquitous growls
Blood manifests like cream
Livelihood stolen through the teeth

Put your purple lipstick on
Inching closer to dawn
You look so marvelous
Almost as radiant as the trees

Ten

The color of my favorite song
Periwinkle fading into orange
A gooey feeling never wrong
Turned on when it rises dawn

Nodes of a fairy child
Little innocence running wild
Future falling for chamomile
London in airy Gibson field

Multi-instrumentalism grooves
Strawberry sublime fruits
This melody so cool
Adding in piano and flutes

5:44am

And in moments like these
When I'm awake and can't sleep
I look at you softly
Wondering, what are your dreams?

Soul World

Unfolding enveloped missiles of soul
Recall senses sadly
Mirage like soft blue-like lanterns below
To light the way gladly

Whether whistling heaven's clouds disappear
The wind dwindles memory

Feel flows

REM

Goodnight stars
Shining in the sky
Venus and Mars
It's time to close my eyes

Drifting into dreamland
Where reading doesn't exist
Shifting into another dimension
Here come the misfits

Flying among the birds
The walls are getting shaky
Not again, is it her?
Please don't wake me

Awake from my mind stories
I miss where I can go
But I don't have to worry
There's always tomorrow

Pool Day

A summers plea
Completely boxed and empty
Drying out the sheets
Of the ongoing insanity

The heat rises
Leaves demises
Creating something of
Different shapes and sizes

Turning the page
Leaving popsicles backstage
For they have melted
Upon her ribcage

Grocery

I dreamt of you last night
And I was happy to see your face
But something didn't feel right
And I had to leave that place

In my dream I wanted you to notice me
My happiness, my growth
I was in line at the grocery
And then you began to approach

I woke up before we exchanged any words
And I laid there wondering
I didn't want to relive hurt
My mind armored protecting me

Pt. 2

In my sleep I see you again
I promise I didn't ask for this
But it was my chance to show you
Who I really am

I don't drink anymore
I told you and you asked what for?
It doesn't suit me
Out of life I want more

This life I have created
No longer needing you to save it
You can watch from the sidelines
Let me enjoy what I have painted

Honey

Dreaming at any moment
Awake or asleep

I'll dream
I'll dream

I'll dream of you bunny

Pearls

And then told me

"It's time to go
In an elusive dream
Just you and me"

The seashells in our sticks
Roaring by all the pink ladies
Who deemed us crazy

Superman sunshines
Ever so often cries
This dream
So I've dreamed
For an eternity

Until now,
It became a reality

June

8,17

The humans won't get it
Black dagger on my arm
Rolls Royce is now finished
The best is yet to come

Heartbeat

Your words floating on a sound wave

Telling me you love me

I promise I'll behave

Kiss

He held my warm hand
While his soft lips danced
I admired his beauty
Our beautiful romance

Crunchy leaves
Right under the trees
Sun waving goodbye
While the moon silently creeps

Our love language is love

Glitter

Tiny little moments
Embodied in my mind
I may never have said this
But you are one of a kind

Like a sparkle on my cheek
Electrifying when you kiss me
Flooded with emotion
Waves crashing over me

Thank you for showing me

That I am lovable and worthy

Consumption

Your voice
Is the first thing that
Captured you inside of my mind

Then your thoughts

Then you

All of
You

Puzzle Piece

I stored you in my locket
Dangling right next to my heart
Because truly you are it
And I cannot fathom being apart

Searching for you for so long
Weeding out the incomplete
I'm glad the others were wrong
And you picked me up off my feet

You are my missing piece
Full of wonders and awe
And now the puzzle is complete
And the storm has finally calmed

Here, Now

I looked in his eyes
Said you don't have to worry
Together as one

Things are okay with you

Stitch

When he tells me
'Look at the moon'
And it's only
Three in the afternoon
It's like I've been waiting for him
To sew up my wounds

Pillow

I want to take a dreamless nap in your arms
Quiet, smooth, and warm

Gruene

You asked me to take a road trip on Saturday
Take me anywhere as long as it's with you
I wish we could just hit replay
And watch this moment after its through

Winding roads on the grassy hillside
I look at you with so much care
A gentleman and you don't even try
With your cowboy hat and messy hair

Lovely dinner by the river
It's cold and you hand me your coat
Inching closer and closer
Nostalgic root beer floats

falling in love

I wish you could view

your elegant soul

through mine

Epitome

noun
1. a person or thing that is a perfect
   example of a particular quality or type
2. a summary of a written work; an abstract

When he told me
It was the time of the sunset
I wandered towards

Wondering if
The sunset
Or he
Was the epitome
Of beauty

June 20

I think I'm falling in love with you
It's so scary but at the same time true
And when I close my eyes
Every dream you make your debut

Laying in your arms it just feels right
No feelings I am willing to fight
Allowing my heart to make the choices
It's you I think of at night

When you tell me you are proud
That I am beautiful when no one is around
I trust your words
But I'm nervous to say them back out loud

I promise I will soon
Give me a little time to make room
I'll open all of me
Just like that little butterfly cocoon

So just please remember
When we are sitting quietly together
And I go to hold your hand
I want to hold it forever

Soft

Do you see my heartbeat?
Can you hear my cheeks turn pink?
The rush you give me
Our melody is so in sync

Your presence brings this calm
I've never felt before until now
It just feels right
Me being nestled in your arms

A picnic under the trees
Please don't ever leave
Without you
As you bite into another cherry

I can't believe you know this song

                    Go ahead and put it on

10:38pm

In a moments notice
You'll be gone
Can we just sit right here
It doesn't have to be for long

Equation

You've created a beautiful memory
Time and time again
Things I softly smile to
Because things are just simple
Like two plus two
Four plus four
I was always good at math
But I think I'm better at loving you

It's always been you

July

Lost

I want to go home
Where is my home?
I thought it was you
But now you are gone
Where do I go now?

Drifting

Train tracks to eclipse
Motorized by heavy ships
Constructed of dark metal
Sinking in her hips

Renewed for another
Pain's younger brother
A ripple effect
To take you down under

Shovel

Lost from this loss
A piece of me is missing
Believing the only solution was
To no longer be living

We could be back together
The next life we could live
There's way too much pressure
Motivation depleted and killed

Can you hear me?
I am desperately crying
Are you watching over me?
If you are, I'll start trying

I'll do this for you
You beautiful soul
Believe it 'til it's true
Somehow find my way out of this hole

Which Pain?

The physical weight
That I can manage
But this emotional pain
Gone beyond damage

Thunderstorm

This rain feels like home
Under the earth crying alone
I quietly sit in the sadness
Saved a seat on her throne

Raindrops or tears?
Both incapsulate fear
It doesn't even matter
I'd rather just disappear

The weight of the water
In a pool surrounded of shadows
Screams drowning my brain
And it's only getting louder

I carefully hold my hand out
Feeling the insanity of the drought
Collection of cries
It has gotten so loud

Swallow

The nightmares came back
Again under attack
Searching for you
And then everything went black

A fear of loss
Of a constant chaos
Take another pill
To abandon all thoughts

Addicted To You

Raindrops long overdue
Withering next to you
Craving an intensity
Give me anything, something new

A blank slate
Or pure heart
It feels tarnished
Torn apart

I'll call until you answer
No one knows me better
I can't run anymore
But still go back to the cancer

The Struggle

Currently constructed in a chainlink
Feeling like I can't move or think

Like I'm just stuck in this quicksand
Yearning to get back to land

Why is it such a struggle to feel a sense of joy
Every ounce of dopamine destroyed

I told the devil he can say hi
Anything but this to make me feel alive

Manuscript

I haven't cried for so long
Numbness permeating my skull
Feels like I am forgotten
Like I'm acting in some role

The script of a sad story
I'm still here acting
Don't do this for me
We're no longer laughing

Move a little to the left
Tilt your head
I don't remember the rest
I just want to go to bed

Pain

Time heals wounds
Unless those wounds are never tended to
Deep blood in the background
Falling open, crying under the full moon

Lonely encompassed by the stars
Wondering which one is you
That day I wished I answered your call
Oblivious of all the pain you were going through

Reading bleak pages without your kitty scribbles
That nickname for just you and me
Pinches and Cheetos in the middle
Scrolling the pictures of us under that one tree

Thats all I really have left
The memories and your letters
A best friend that came and went
Now just me lost in my own shadow

Fable

Fables you tell yourself
That drugs are okay for your health
Thinking no one is watching
Or cares
That you will never be enough

Resting the bottle under your pillow
Friendships mutilated and shallow
So lonely
Lost
Sleeping next to your so called hero

You wake up and do it again
Live in a constant clouded perception
Angry at the world
Cold
Surrounded by all of your messes

This doesn't have to be your life
It's time to live like you are alive
You're desperate
Dying
I can see it in your eyes

Grief

Five letters that devour
An unwavering loss that I feel
Sitting curled in the cold shower
Desperately wishing this was not real

Walking this lonely Earth without you
No laugh has ever been the same
Only me in this two person canoe
Will I ever experience joy again?

It has now been two years
I still feel lost, blindly living
At times I do feel that you are near
Then grief restarts back to the beginning

I am told painful feelings need to be felt
So tomorrow less heartache will invade
Dry off with the towel from the shelf
And put back on my mask in this masquerade

If only you knew

Trinket

Isolation on this lonely sailboat
In the middle of absolutely no where
Tipping and barely staying afloat
Without even the slightest care

Best friends with depression
Consumed in this thick cloud
Hope paper thin
Always wearing a deep frown

I guess I'll just keep sailing
On the ocean of lost tears
For so long its been raining
Droplets of glum souvenirs

Jump

Pink dye
Saturating thoughts
Helmet of hope
Faster, the roots will rot

A will to no longer live
Nothing left but bottles of regret
Blood was not enough
I just wanted to forget

Picking up the pieces
A trail uncovered from the balcony
Desperately crying inside
With a U-Haul behind me

Grim Reaper

Perhaps it shows
While my sadness explodes
But I hide it softly
So no one knows

A smiling face
Too pretty to erase
This fake story
I've had to embrace

Completely lost identity
Conformed entity
Soul so broken
Shattered and empty

So when the time comes
And it's no longer fun
Death with greet me
I'll be okay when it's done

If you turned to this page
Just know it'll be okay

August

Bomb

She opened her eyes
Unsure of his cries
Infidelity caught
In his soul and his lies

Was she not good enough
Did she break, was she tough
I must go, she said
I am about to erupt

August 5

Thoughts?
I have absolutely none
Mustered in a box
I've been long gone

My truth is my haven
Where has that led me
Because all you have taken
Is my beloved sanity

Rippled with fear
Of you walking out that door
Might as well cut me with your shears
And leave me dying on the floor

To Him

I had to walk away
Somber every single day
I still braided your hair
But it all began in May

Your physical being
Translucently reeling
My profound blindness
For how you were feeling

Now looking back
At all this and that
You never really cared
I was simply a doormat

A manipulation king
Painting something I had always dreamed
When in reality
Your cold eyes began to sing

I still danced the dance
Because my love for you was so immense
Pure intentions
Got muddled by chance

God, you meant the world to me
And writing this I'm starting to see
I have so much to give
I can't wait to make someone else happy

Ashes

I took many pictures to remember this
Somehow I knew my mind would want to erase it

I was delusional and didn't know back then
That my fireplace would eventually consume them

Gust

Radio silence
Locked into the abyss
Pouring out violence
Streaming in benevolence

I told myself
That I would be better
So I took it from the shelf
And tore up your letter

Meaningless words
Thrown in the wind
Among all the birds
And all of your sins

Weeds

The lies you tell me
They finally caught up to you
I know you are struggling
But I can't sit here and wait for you

I can't save you from the sadness
From the pain of your mistakes
The hope, you have to grab it
Please grab it before it breaks

It's unfair to you and me
If I promise that I will be here
I have to keep healing
I don't know how to make it any more clear

I will sit on the sidelines
Silently cheering you on
And hopefully in time
You can one day prove me wrong

In Time

I told you I would always love you
That you have a special place in my heart
This was months after we were through
I needed to move on and have a fresh start

It still isn't easy
Everything in me believed you were the one
I imagined us starting a family
You playing ice hockey with our son

I know we both were not perfect
Something beautiful turned into pain
If it really is worth it
We would see each other again

The universe will show me
I can't force love to keep loving
You'll come back if it's meant to be
This wasn't all meant for nothing

Devils Advocate

Once you were a stranger
Sitting in a bar
Two years later
And here we are

I no longer know your favorite color
Or what you like to do
Simply back to a stranger
I once never knew

I Wish I Told You

I miss you
This feeling hurts my heart
Like the dagger on your arm
Before you left
I wish I told you

I wish I told you
All of the things I love
What reminds me of you
How many times my phone rings
And I am hoping it is you

I wish I told you
Anytime anything good or bad happens
I just want to tell you
Laugh and cry with you
We are so good at laughing

I wish I told you
How much you truly mean to me
From the depth of my being
How I look at the moon
And wonder if you are looking too

I wish I told you
I stare at the stars
Laying on the soft grass
Hoping one starts shooting across the sky
And I can wish on forever

I wish I told you
You don't have to be scared
That we can take on the world
Make a beautiful life
And get that ranch you dream of

I wish I told you
I tell my friends about you
How much fun we have
When we do absolutely nothing
Those are my favorite moments

I wish I told you
That I was scared to fall in love with you
Because the thought of losing you

heartbreak

Was enough to stop me
But I stopped listening

I wish I told you
How I have never told anyone else some things
And I trust you with every ounce
Because you listen
And that took a lot from me

I wish I told you
I am in love with you
And that I am ready
To begin creating our life
Just us two

I wish I told you
I want you to come back
I don't want the thought of losing you
To be true
I miss you

Say Goodbye

I believe
It is all meant to be
Even though I went back
I finally knew it was time to leave

If we ended up together
I would have been aching and disheveled
And then my life
Wouldn't have gotten any better

There truly is a reason for it all
I'm so glad I didn't answer your call
I was never perfect
And it's okay if again I fall

Padlock

You told me you never loved me
That I was unimportant and unworthy

I believed every single word
And coming from you, that really hurt

But that's all I ever knew;
Like how to tie my shoes

I truly thought you were the one
Like how the moon desperately needs the sun

Now returning to therapy
For it you made fun of me

I begin to understand
And my self-love has started to expand

I forgive you
For all of the pain you tried so hard to glue

At least I don't cry anymore
And have finally shut that heavy door

Rain

Just when I was starting to get over you
Not yet, you said
And you did what you always do

Crept back into my mind
Sent a simple text
For the second time

I already told you goodbye
This life I've made
You don't deserve a reply

Henry Slade

We haven't talked in five months, but in those five months I've accomplished so much. I thought of you a few times, but then I come back here in this notebook to write down all of my feelings and thoughts. All of my pain. All of my growth. I'm so sick of only thinking about the good times because in those good times there still was pain. Pain hidden behind the laughs, the love, the dancing, the smiles. Pain was so heavy but invisible and it's like it didn't even exist, but it did. And now I realize you think you were the only one that experienced pain but that's probably because I hid my pain so well.

I've been so good at hiding my pain for so long. I just don't want to be a burden. The pain hidden behind the way I tug at my necklaces, the reason I always need to go out dancing so I can sweat out the pain and the memories that I don't want to remember. I hide my pain so well.

I hide my pain so well I can't even find it. Like my black cat on the sea of the black jeans, the black sweaters, the black leather jackets, the black T-shirts that are lying on the floor of my closet. Where is he? I call his name and only see his green eyes. Does he want to be seen or is he enjoying hiding? Being invisible unless he is sought out? Is he my pain? He sleeps with me every night nestled in my arms. Is he healing my pain? Is he taking away all of those dreadful memories of me pushing my pain away? The memories I have of me putting myself last only so I can heal you. I wake up a little happier each day with cat hair all over my face and a little less pain from yesterday.

P.S.

I just want to run to you
And I hope you know that every time I don't
I almost do

heartbreak

I blew out the candle
To get the last smell of you

September

Letters

Why is it so hard to talk about love
For myself and how I show up
Something so foreign
Completely abandoned and shoved

This can't be the shortest chapter
That would be something of a disaster
I guess I'll keep writing
Faster and faster

Unfolding

So I press another flower
Trying my best to hold on to this
I wish time moved a bit slower
So my soul could truly be kissed

I press to keep
To eventually let go
That doesn't make me weak
Blossom into a rose

Diary

I'm sorry I haven't written in a while
Mind jumbled with unwritten thoughts
Life moves fast sometimes I'm in denial
Forgot everything I should have brought

These moments to stop
Eyelids shut and mind open
Remembering you used to take up a whole lot
Now just a little spec in the ocean

For Today

I stop comparing myself to others
Only compare me to myself yesterday
I want to choose a different color
Asking for any happiness to stay

I know that there are highs
With that come the lows
It doesn't hurt to at least try
And be a better person than before

Loving yourself brings love to her
She may need it more than you do
Envision her as that little girl
Before conformity began to accrue

Today I allow myself to be
Exhibit love instead of hate
Hug a stranger in the streets
Before I realize it's too late

self

Here you go pretty thing

Vase Of

Pink baby peonies
Royal red roses
Wispy white carnations
Three gladioluses
And one eucalyptus

Gentle
Gentle
Gentle

I remind myself

Alone But Not Lonely

I am not missing anything
I am home
I don't need another silver ring
Or another sweater for the cold

I don't need another person to love
To have next to me laying in bed
I don't need anything else
That I don't already have

Sometimes when I am walking in nature alone
I think about the person
Who should be walking them with me
But all I need is me

3:12am

It had to end there
When you called that one night
I didn't answer

Little Darling

Drawing circles with my toes
Childlike in this flow
A little happy baby
Never letting her go

Love your younger self
You have no one else
Be kind to her
So that everything else can melt

September 10

She looks at herself
Admiring all of her wealth
Her bravery and resilience
A story that she rarely tells

Now it wasn't that easy
A lot of loss and pain she had to see
But her earned confidence
Floats within her so freely

Self-love is underrated

Affirmation

I look at you and begin to smile
We've been doing this thing called life for a while

All I've truly got is you
After everything we have been through

I promise to give you more grace
And stack more love upon the messy bookcase

Because this mirror shows pure beauty
In the reflection it has always been me

Tall

Empowered, dangerous, majestic
Confident, delicate, rebellious

Qualities of powerful women
Me being one of them

Let Her Go

Attempting to translate her self love
Having to finally say that this is enough
She deserves so much better
Bombarding her is not what she wants

Please don't take advantage of her kind heart
Repair took a while after she was torn apart
She begs to let her free
All the tears she has already mopped

If respect was at hand
Then you would listen and understand
This is about her dreams and peace
Not you being her man

Paintbrush

A floor of painted crystals
The moon waving to her
Wind like a whistle
Her heart like a purr

Youth imagined quaint
Childlike dancing in between
A smile one could only paint
Beauty flowing out as a beam

You Are You

Not one being should have the power
To diminish your intrinsic value
For it is far beyond beautiful

You deserve
Not just the world
But the whole universe

October

7:14am

Little by little
The sun shined
Opening her arms
Hello sky

Press Pause

A pollution of thoughts run wild
Trying to grasp a sort of sanity
Why don't you love me?
I can't control everything
Trying my best to be kind, be compassionate
Can't you see I'm at least trying?
Judgment struck from the wand above
Hate diminished from the inner skeleton
We have our bones, our blood
But do we have the willingness to truly love?
In this life we have to do right
The humans constantly being demolished
The animals crying out for help
The flowers withering to the ground
All we have left is our mind
Even that hasn't been enough
Take a step back
Look around you
See the faces of others
Is it a mirrored reflection?
Do you see what I see?
Because what I see is spoiled beauty
We must do better

Birds

Poetry hidden in the shadows
Becoming free
Just as it should be

Seeds

I planted you a tree
Do you want to come and see?

It already has so much beauty
Just like you and me

Animals

I'll make some room
In this butterfly fantasy
One for you
And one for me

Strolling on this spirit walk
In comes this cave
They were fluttering right on top
Painting out your name

Hug

I pause to listen
To the flowing breeze
Watching the water glisten
Doves flying out the trees

Nature is my mother
Gratitude for this magic
I politely hug her
So she can be freed from her sadness

A crying planet
Of mankind madness
Maybe I can save it
To get back to a sense of bliss

We Are

We are nature
Roots of wisdom and life
Trunk filled with guidance and hope
Branches holding connection of love
Leaves flowing out emotion and energy

You are strong
Can withstand any storm
Allow yourself to flow with the wind
Give others your abundance
For it is already given by our Earth

nature

I love you

October 8

Slowly now
Your cucumber smile will show itself
And the piano keys will dance
I hope you don't stop skipping across the
pond
This is your chance

Blueberry sky says hi
Rays surrounding Garrison
Bubbles keep floating
It is here and everlasting

Harness of happiness
In the wild sea of dreams
Melancholy grasses
Miscounted, make believe

Humid

So many complain
Humidity is hot
Sticky

Perspective unraveling
Fuels my skin
Comfort

Nature's own blanket
Listen to the mist
Damp

She holds me
Pressed flowers
Comfort

Heater

It's cold but the sun warms me
While my polite thoughts start entering

Its a new day to not think about you
Under clear skies oh so blue

Blank canvas on my white pants
They may get dirty as I dance

Now, it is time to put my pen down
So I can admire the trees that have grown

October 19

When I open my eyes
My cat curled by my side
Noticing the sun's rays beaming
A comfortable silence
What will today bring me?
A fantasy of only things I have dreamed

Immense gratitude for everything I have
This pen, this paper
The ability to breathe
I always wondered what brought me here
But some things are left unknown
Excitement in this mystery

My favorite song turns on
The mood of something of a lullaby
This is how it begins
My feet land on the floor
Awaking my body with a kiss
Taking on the day just for today

I disconnect to connect
With nature and the flowers
This beauty of exploding magic
Sometimes I forget
To thank her for showing up
A little goes a long way

A walk in the park
Just right down the street
I am greeted with leaves and smiles
The playful children laughing
Clouds softly moving by
Taking in all of the wonders I sometimes miss

A hug from the wind
She has said her goodbyes
It's now time to walk back
A different path for new time
I thank her for this moment
Oh, what a beautiful day

Nature Shower

I am committed to growth
Deep in the trees I know
Whispers of tranquility
Promises on the radio

Troubleshooting all of the noise
Rebooting consistency void
This newness kept
I used to think I had a choice

My voice is becoming louder
The strength is persistent
Taking a lot of love showers
Saying goodbye to the serpent

Mulch

Glistening dirt
Nuance of hurt
Cabinet of pride
Poetic first

October 23

It is a green day
The perfect time to forage
No more time for you

November

Check Please

I asked myself out on a date
And she said of course,
But only if you pay

Can I tell you a secret?

He doesn't deserve you

Identity

I am beginning to grasp that happiness is true
Fulfillment in my skin carved into my tattoo

She must protect her precious energy now
Only radiant positivity allowed

An identity whole and becoming complete
A lovely woman one day I'm sure you'll meet

11:27am

Persona unfolding like a blooming rose
It is I that I finally chose

Quieter streets and lessened fights
Arguments in my mind begin to rewrite

Viewing insanity through a new lens
Camera clicks without contends

Bodies

The world
But a canvas

Life
The art

My body
The paintbrush

I just want to paint

New

Sprinkled melody of fortune
Yellow daisies in the jar
Food for the soul
Leaving crystals out to charge

Harmony of soft peace
Feelings of joy again
Letting sadness release
No longer broken

So I pick a few more flowers
To fill the clear vase
Taking back my power
If I have to, just in case

6:21 am

A total of twelve tulips
Sitting next to my bed
No longer having to prove it
There is peace in my head

I tried for so long
To be what everyone needed
Always feeling alone
This cycle constantly repeated

Until this one time
When I opened to a page
Animals and protectors combined
A jellyfish had a lot to say

Rebirth is here
Wisdom of the universe
Breathing in fulfilling air
Leaving the old in my purse

Connect deeper with your heart
The jellyfish said
You're the best piece of art
Admire the tulips by your bed

Queen

Your majesty
You are but a delight
A creature of electricity
Radiant and just right

pressed flowers

Shanti
Shanti
Shanti

November 21

Hugged by this tile
Bathtub of vulnerability
Curtained by a smile
Delight of comfortability

Moment with myself
Soft beats on the side
I'd choose this above all else
Having nothing to hide

Farm

A little lamb once told me
       Don't break the peace
              Then I realized
My peace is the one I keep

Intuition

Red ink;
Hypnotizing
I'm locked in
Cherries gliding right past me

Flames and obvious smoke
The stop sign appears
Warnings loudly spoke
Leaving it all on the stairs

Liberated from your apple
Dissolved your crunch
I'd rather go to the doctor
Put myself first for once

Piano

And in that moment

      With the vibrations of the fluidity

            I realized that I

   Am one with the keys

Blossom

Every thorn that jutted out to touch me
All of the days I slowly bled out for you
It was all worth the sorrow I did not foresee
Onto the world I embarked anew

She embodied true magic

Saved

The mysterious nature
Of her soft fluid walk
An ambient creature
Borrowing unrevealed thoughts

She only shows a little
Then retracts in her nook
You get a glimpse of her shimmer
Again hiding behind her book

She knew what she needed
Sitting right there on top
Becoming undefeated
Letting out her teardrops

She's no longer afraid
Of you and your notions
Allowed herself to be saved
By the divine patient devotion

I hope you dance